World of Islam

Islam, Law, and Human Rights

MASON CREST PUBLISHERS
PHILADELPHIA

World of Islam

World of Islam

Islam, Law, and Human Rights

ANNA MELMAN

Editorial Consultants: Foreign Policy Research Institute, Philadelphia, PA

Mason Crest Publishers
370 Reed Road
Broomall, PA 19008
www.masoncrest.com

First printing

1 3 5 7 9 8 6 4 2

Library of Congress Cataloging-in-Publication Data

Melman, Anna.
  Islam, law and human rights / Anna Melman.
      p. cm. — (World of Islam)
  ISBN 978-1-4222-1362-9 (hardcover)
  ISBN 978-1-4222-1365-0 (pbk.)
  1. Human rights—Islamic countries—Juvenile literature. 2. Human rights—Religious aspects—Islam—
Juvenile literature. 3. Islamic law—Juvenile literature. 4. Human rights—Juvenile literature. I. Title.
  KBP2460.M45 2006
  342.16708'5—dc22
                              2008054298

Anna Melman is deputy editor at the Global Research in International Affairs (GLORIA) Center. She is
also assistant editor of the *Turkish Studies* journal and of the *Middle East Review of International
Affairs (MERIA) Journal*.

Table of Contents

Defining Human Rights

Human rights are the rights that we are deemed to possess simply by virtue of the fact that we are human. Most societies agree that these basic rights include the right to live freely and to believe what one chooses. But the definition of human rights can vary based on the historic practice, religion, or government of a region. Certain groups of people have their own interpretations of what constitutes basic human rights.

In Western societies and—in theory if not always in practice—around the world in general, a consensus has developed over time on what basic human rights are. The Western idea of human rights is contained in such materials as British common law, the U.S. Declaration of Independence and the U.S. Constitution (including the Bill of Rights), and the French Revolution's Declaration of the Rights of Man and of the Citizen. This Western viewpoint has been universalized in many international treaties,

In the United States and other Western countries, certain human rights and freedoms are guaranteed by law. In many countries influenced by Islamic law, however, human rights are defined differently.

laws in many countries, and the United Nation's Universal Declaration of Human Rights.

In countries where Islam is the majority religion, however, human rights are defined differently. Islam is a monotheistic religion founded during the seventh century on the Arabian Peninsula by the Prophet Muhammad, who was both a religious and political leader. In the West, separation between a secular public sphere and a religious private sphere is a basic framework for society. In Muslim majority states, Islam prescribes both secular and religious duties through Islamic law, called Sharia.

Historically, Muslim majority countries have not been consistent in how they implement Sharia within their governments

Islam

Islam is a religion that emerged from the Arabian Peninsula between 622 and 632 C.E. It is based on the teachings of a prophet named Muhammad, who united the Arab tribes under his rule.

The word *Islam* is derived from the Arabic verb *aslama*, which means "to submit." Muhammad taught his followers that they must submit themselves to the will of Allah (or God). Muhammad's followers became known as Muslims, or "those who submit."

Muslims believe that the word of God was given to Muhammad through the angel Gabriel in a series of revelations. After Muhammad's death in 632, these revelations were written down in the Qur'an, the Muslim holy book.

Muhammad's successors, who served as the faith's chief civil and religious leaders, were called caliphs. Disagreement over how caliphs were to be chosen led to the development of two main branches of the religion—Sunni Islam and Shia Islam. The majority of Muslims (85 percent) are Sunnis.

and how they deal with human rights. Leaders have varied from identifying human rights as a priority, to giving the issues lip service, to ignoring Islamic law. And of course, too, while there is a general consensus in Muslim majority countries over the terms of Islamic law, there are also variations and debates among different schools and interpretations of Islam.

This situation is further complicated by the rise of political Islamism, which rejects any law not based on Sharia. Since Islamists tend to view their interpretation of Islam as the only proper one, this idea is often expressed as a refusal to accept legislation made by human beings. Political Islamists are a minority, albeit a powerful one in Muslim majority states and an important force even where Muslims live as a minority. However, a large number of Muslims support the idea that Islamic law be given priority in setting the rules for their government and society. A 2008 report found that 66 percent of Egyptians, 60 percent of Pakistanis, and 54 percent of Jordanians say that Sharia should be the only source of legislation in their countries.

What Are Human Rights?

At their core, human rights are the rights to life, freedom, equality before the law, and justice. Human rights are considered to be universal and therefore are for all people, no matter where they live and no matter what religion, gender, or race they are. Human rights are also considered indivisible, meaning that they must all exist together because if one right is denied that loss will affect all other rights. Even in countries where human rights are overwhelmingly upheld, it took many centuries for governments to reach today's understanding and respect for human rights.

While human rights are guaranteed by law in all Western countries and many Third World nations today, there are countries in which people continue to struggle to achieve these basic

Members of this crowd of Muslims in London are holding signs to protest supposed incidents of discrimination against their religion. In most predominantly Muslim countries, however, it would be impossible for a religious minority such as Christians or Jews to publicly protest against mistreatment.

rights. But even in places where human rights are not protected to the same degree, they are still given lip service. In other words, there is no explicitly expressed alternative system or open rejection of human rights as defined in the West, but simply the fact that this admitted ideal is not put into practice. It is only in Muslim majority states that one can find a large body of opinion and even governments—as in Iran and Saudi Arabia, for example—that put forward an altogether different model.

Historical Development in the West

The concept of human rights as a coherent political and philosophical approach is relatively new in human history and evolved very slowly over time. It took many centuries, revolutions, thinkers, wars, suffering and executions, and individual courageous campaigners to reach the modern notion of human rights.

The idea of certain rights was not unknown to the Ancient Jews, Greeks, and Romans, but the concept was very different from that of today. A belief in the natural or God-given laws of the universe led to a concept of "natural rights." However, this certainly did not mean that people were equal or free. For example, slavery was also seen as a natural part of the universe and people were often treated in very cruel and unjust ways.

It was not until the 13th century, in England, that a legal document established certain rights of citizens. In 1215, King John of England was forced by his country's nobility to sign the Magna Carta, the Great Charter of Freedoms. The Magna Carta did not guarantee anything close to what are understood today as human rights, but it did give the king's subjects certain rights under British common law. They included such important matters as the right to inherit property and protection from excessive taxes. The document even proclaimed the king to be subject to the law. The Magna Carta

King John of England signs the Magna Carta—an agreement made in 1215 in which the king agreed to respect certain rights of the nobles and of free citizens, as well as to rule according to laws on which the people agreed. The Magna Carta is considered an important first step in the development of modern Western-style democracy.

was therefore a fundamental step in the development of a system of rights enshrined in law and protected by institutions.

Revolutions and Rights

Two revolutions during the 18th century spurred important developments in the notion of the rights of people. One occurred when the 13 colonial governments in North America declared themselves independent from the British Empire, launching the American Revolutionary War (1775–1783). The 1776 Declaration of Independence was a key expression of the rights and equality of all people. Its preamble stated: "We hold these truths to be self-evident; that all men are created equal, that they are endowed by their creator with certain unalienable rights, that among these are life, liberty and the pursuit of happiness."

In 1789, two years after the Constitution of the United States was adopted, 10 amendments known as the Bill of Rights were proposed. The amendments were made in order to secure the support of those who initially opposed the Constitution and feared an over-powerful federal government. This series of articles was another important step in securing the rights of citizens: The First Amendment guaranteed the freedom of speech, of religion, and of the press, as well as the right of assembly. The Fourth Amendment regulated the rights of the authorities to search people and seize their property. The Fifth Amendment provided due process of law, guaranteeing that people could be tried only once for an alleged crime. The Sixth and Seventh Amendments promised the right to a speedy trial and trial by jury. The Eighth forbade "cruel and unusual punishment."

In Europe, the French Revolution (1789–1799) was inspired by American principles as well as by ideas that had been developing in France over the previous century. The revolution resulted in the overthrow of a monarchy and establishment of a republic, or government by the people. It was in this revolutionary context that the Declaration of the Rights of Man and of the Citizen was produced in 1789. It stated: "Men are born free and equal in rights . . . [including] liberty, property, security and resistance to oppression."

While such rights were being written into the law books, thinkers were also exploring the concept of human rights. Philosopher Thomas Paine responded to critics of the French Revolution by publishing *The Rights of Man* (1791), a pamphlet in which he argued that all men were entitled to political rights because of their "natural" equality in the eyes of God.

Restrictions and Exceptions

Still, many countries of the world did not recognize this concept of human rights. But even in countries that had written human rights protection into laws, there were certain groups of people for whom these laws did not apply.

Slavery was legal in Great Britain until 1833 and in the United States until 1865. Until the 1800s property ownership in Great Britain was a requirement for eligibility to vote. It was not until 1921 in the United States and 1928 in Britain that women received the vote on equal terms to men. In the United

During the 18th century, many people in Europe and North America came to believe that humans are endowed with "unalienable rights." However, despite the influence of philosophers and freethinkers during this Age of Enlightenment, certain groups of people—such as these African slaves—were not considered to have the same basic rights as others.

States the civil rights movement of the 1950s brought to the attention of the world the fact that black Americans were being denied even the most basic rights. Amendments to the U.S. Constitution would guarantee some of these human rights. They would bar slavery, reinforce the rights of all people to equal treatment, and guarantee the right to vote for women.

During the first half of the 20th century dictatorships took power in some countries and revoked earlier rights. This occurred in Fascist Italy during the 1920s and Nazi Germany in the 1930s. Other places, notably the Union of Soviet Socialist Republics (Soviet Union), proclaimed broad rights in laws and constitutions, but never implemented them.

The Universal Declaration of Human Rights

The United Nations is an international organization founded after the Second World War (1939–1945) to promote peace among countries throughout the world. In response to the horrors of World War II and the crimes of fascism, the UN drew up an international document to establish standards and norms of human rights. Members of the UN General Assembly voted to adopt the Universal Declaration of Human Rights on December 10, 1948.

The preamble of the UN declaration states that all people are entitled to the rights laid out in its 30 articles. Although the document was not binding on the member countries, it stated, "human rights should be protected by the rule of law." The declaration also stated that none of the rights could be taken away from people. The adoption of this document was an enormously important step in the establishment of human rights. The articles of the UN declaration became an international standard for protecting human rights and for judging cases in which such rights had been violated.

Excerpts from the Universal Declaration of Human Rights

Article 1. All human beings are born free and equal in dignity and rights. . . .

Article 2. Everyone is entitled to all the rights and freedoms . . . without distinction of any kind, such as race, color, sex, language, religion, political or other opinion, national or social origin, property, birth or other status. . . .

Article 3. Everyone has the right to life, liberty and security of person.

Article 4. No one shall be held in slavery or servitude; slavery and the slave trade shall be prohibited in all their forms.

Article 5. No one shall be subjected to torture or to cruel, inhuman or degrading treatment or punishment.

Article 6. Everyone has the right to recognition everywhere as a person before the law.

Article 7. All are equal before the law and are entitled without any discrimination to equal protection of the law. . . .

Article 9. No one shall be subjected to arbitrary arrest, detention or exile. . . .

Article 11. Everyone charged with a penal offence has the right to be presumed innocent until proved guilty according to law in a public trial at which he has had all the guarantees necessary for his defense . . .

Article 16. (1) Men and women of full age, without any limitation due to race, nationality or religion, have the right to marry and to found a family. They are entitled to equal rights as to marriage, during marriage and at its dissolution. (2) Marriage shall be entered into only with the free and full consent of the intending spouses. . . .

Article 18. Everyone has the right to freedom of thought, conscience and religion; this right includes freedom to change his religion or belief, and freedom . . .to manifest his religion or belief in teaching, practice, worship and observance.

Article 19. Everyone has the right to freedom of opinion and expression. . . .

Article 21. (1) Everyone has the right to take part in the government of his country, directly or through freely chosen representatives. . . .

Article 25. (1) Everyone has the right to a standard of living adequate for the health and well-being of himself and of his family, including food, clothing, housing and medical care and necessary social services . . .

Article 26. (1) Everyone has the right to education. Education shall be free, at least in the elementary and fundamental stages. . . .

A young girl cooks a meal in Lahore, Pakistan, 1979. That year—designated by the United Nations the "International Year of the Child,"—studies showed that there were about 56 million children under the age of 15 who were working, and that many of them were exploited. In response, the UN prepared the Convention on the Rights of the Child. This international agreement was signed in 1989.

International Conventions

Various international conventions have dealt with the issue of human rights. A convention is an agreement among states that governments are obligated by law to implement once it is ratified—once the agreement has been confirmed by the legislative body of the state. A convention focuses on a specific area and sets more detailed standards than a declaration does.

When the UN General Assembly adopts a convention, it establishes international standards. Some UN human rights conventions include the Convention Against Torture (1985), Convention on the Elimination of All Forms of Discrimination Against Women (1979), and Convention on the Rights of the Child (1989).

Sharia Law

The system of Islamic law, or Sharia, literally means "path" or "path to the water source." Muslims consider Sharia to be God's commandments toward living a life that will ultimately lead to salvation, both for the individual and society. It is seen as having been revealed through divine signs interpreted by human beings.

Sharia is supposed to govern all aspects of life, providing a framework for the regulation of everything—public and private—including all matters ranging from religion to personal dealings to business relationships. While this system of Islamic law is consistent in essence, it has been interpreted in different ways. In some majority Muslim countries, it has been narrowly restricted to interpretation only by properly trained clerics. In other nations it has been broadened by the rise of governments that frequently ignore Sharia in the formulation of public laws.

Deriving the Law

Sharia comes from a combination of four main sources. They are the Qur'an (the Muslim holy book), the *hadith* (the sayings and actions of the prophet Muhammad and his companions), *ijma* (consensus), and *qiyas* (reasoning).

The Qur'an and the hadith are the primary sources of Sharia. Muslims believe the Qur'an to be God's Word transmitted through the Angel Gabriel to the Prophet Muhammad. Islamic tradition holds that the Qur'an was revealed to Muhammad over a period of 23 years. Furthermore, his actions and sayings were recorded in the hadith, which are seen as the second source for the determination of Sharia and to be consulted for matters related to the proper way of life. Beyond those two traditional

The Qur'an, the sacred scriptures of Islam, includes the revelations that Allah is said to have given to Muhammad in the seventh century. Over centuries, a corpus of Islamic law was developed based on the Qur'an as well as stories (hadith) about the example of Muhammad and his early followers.

sources, which are accepted by all branches of Islam, ijma and qiyas are accepted by most Islamic schools of thought as sources from which Sharia is derived.

Ijma refers to scholarly consensus for matters not directly addressed by the Qur'an or hadith. The scholars in question are referred to as *ulama*. According to the Qu'ran, a consensus by a large group of pious people cannot be wrong, and thus, the tradition of ijma was established whereby ulama, using juristic reasoning (*ijtihad*), reached a consensus on certain matters based on principles set out in the Qu'ran and hadith.

Today, however, many Muslims believe that the period of ijtihad is over. What was decided by scholars at a certain time in the past is part of the canon of Islamic law, but today the necessary knowledge and training does not exist for new interpretations that would be binding as law. Interpretation, then, deals with mere details or in evaluating centuries-old sources rather than in breaking any new ground. This approach is in contradiction to reform efforts and thus is under challenge for those who support a broader adaptation of Sharia and Islam itself to the contemporary world.

The fourth source of Sharia is qiyas, or legal analogy (the determination of new practices based on comparisons with past practices). Legal analogy is applied to matters not specifically addressed by the Qur'an and hadith. Such issues were not covered because they were not relevant at the time. (For example, drug use is not referred to in the Qu'ran, but it has been deemed impermissible because of the explicit Qur'anic ban on alcohol.) Qiyas is used by jurists to understand the reasoning behind ideas and laws presented in the revealed sources, allowing rulings on new conditions to be applied aptly and consistently. This must be done, however, within the traditional framework.

Schools of Jurisprudence

The period of time from Muhammad's death in 632 to the Middle Ages (ca. 1100–1450s) saw the development of five major schools of Islamic jurisprudence (theory or philosophy of law), each with its own way of relating to Sharia. The Shia and the four Sunni schools created interpretations of religious law and established binding precedents. Despite differences among the five schools, all are generally accepted as reflecting valid legal interpretations of Islam, and there is a sharing and debating of ideas among them. These schools tended to gain preference based on geography, a situation that still exists today.

The Hanafi school is the oldest and most widespread Sunni legal school. It is favored across the Middle East (with the exception of Arabia) and in lands formerly under Ottoman Turkish rule (including Turkey, Iraq, Syria, and Egypt). It is also widespread among Sunni Muslims in southeastern Europe, Central Asia (including Afghanistan), and the Indian subcontinent (including Pakistan). Abu Hanifa al-Numan ibn Thabit, the school's founder, was the first to use ijma and qiyas as methods for deriving Sharia.

The Shafi'i school is favored primarily in Southeast Asia, and it is the official school followed by the governments in Malaysia and Indonesia. It is the second-largest school of Sunni Islamic jurisprudence, claiming about 28 percent of all Sunni Muslims worldwide as adherents. The Shafi'i school, while accepting all four sources for the derivation of Sharia, emphasizes the rigorous application of legal principles and is said to be among the more conservative of the schools. Unlike the Hanafi school, it does not leave room for private judgment in the derivation of legal principles.

The third-largest Sunni school is Maliki, with 15 percent of Muslims as followers. It is the most prevalent school in North and

West Africa. The Maliki school deviates from the other schools in its sources for deriving Sharia. First, it includes the rulings of what are known as the four rightly guided caliphs—the first four successors of Muhammad—which are not included in the traditional hadiths. Furthermore, Maliki practices rely on the rulings of the *Salaf* (customs of the righteous ancestors) of Medina (the town in today's Saudi Arabia that is the burial place of Muhammad and site of the first mosque). Medinian Salaf is included because the way the people of Medina lived is viewed as how Muhammad lived. When Medinian practice contradicts the accepted hadith, the Maliki school often rules in favor of the Medinian way.

A courtyard at the Mosque of the Prophet in Medina, Saudi Arabia. Muhammad's tomb is located within the mosque; other important figures from the history of Islam are buried nearby. One is Imam Malik ibn Anas (711–795 C.E.), who established the Maliki school of Islamic law.

The smallest Sunni legal school is the Hanbali school, whose rulings are followed mostly in Saudi Arabia and Qatar. It is the school followed by the Wahhabi and Salafi sects of Islam. The school was founded by Imam Ahmad bin Hanbal, who relied on some basic principles of jurisprudence in reference to Sharia. Like the other schools, it relies on the Qur'an and the hadith as the primary sources of law; it never defers to ijma or qiyas when there is a textual reference on the subject available. However, if there was no explicit textual basis for a matter, the verdicts of the companions of Muhammad are considered as being more important than those of the ijma or qiyas of other scholars. If companions had differing opinions, the one supported by the text is to be followed. Only if none of these methods are applicable does this school resort to qiyas, and that source is used very carefully.

Shia Muslims follow the Ja'afari school. The main difference between the Ja'afari school and the Sunni schools is their opinions toward analytical reasoning. The Shia tend to encourage individual ijtihad more than Sunnis do, which gives the leading clerics among them more authority. There are also differences between Sunni and Shia approaches to law regarding matters of personal status (marriage and divorce), religious taxes, inheritance, and commerce.

Since the 19th century some modern scholars have maintained that Muslims do not have to choose a particular Islamic legal school to follow. They urge that new and individual interpretations of Islamic law be made.

Content of Sharia

Muslims believe that Sharia regulates all aspects of life. A person's actions fall within five categories: obligatory, recommended, permitted, disliked, and forbidden. Most human actions fall into the permitted category—acts that are neither encouraged nor discouraged.

Sharia is also commonly divided into four thematic areas: laws relating to personal acts of worship, laws relating to commercial relationships, laws relating to personal status, and penal laws. Some scholars divide Sharia into slightly different categories: laws relating to ritual practice; laws relating to commerce and contracts; laws relating to morals and manners; laws relating to beliefs; and laws relating to punishments. Among the areas governed by Islamic law are dietary behavior; marriage, polygamy, and divorce; inheritance; sports and gambling; acceptable dress; penalties; and apostasy (the renunciation of one's faith).

Islamic law prescribes specific dietary behaviors. It prohibits Muslims from eating or drinking certain foods and drink, including

Chinese butchers in a *halal* meat shop, which sells beef and mutton slaughtered according to Sharia religious guidelines.

In countries governed by Sharia-based laws, men have greater rights than women.

intoxicants, blood, the meat of pigs, and the meat of animals slaughtered in any way other than the one allowed by Sharia.

In establishing rules about personal status, Sharia describes marriage as a contract between a man and a woman in which the man is the family's head and a wife may not act against his wishes. A woman can obtain certain rights by demanding them in her marriage contract. But in many instances—especially in places where Sharia has had an impact on modern law—women's rights are curtailed. According to the Qur'an, men can have up to four wives, and such polygamy is legal in many Islamic countries. However, the practice has been banned in some countries, such as Tunisia and Turkey.

A man can divorce his wife without cause, although he must provide her with a sum of money specified in the marriage contract and permit her to keep her dowry (the property or money she brought to the marriage). The situations in which a woman can divorce her husband are limited, but in some Muslim majority countries, such as Iran and Egypt, laws are in place that give women greater rights in filing for divorce. Women—mothers, wives, and daughters—are guaranteed an inheritance in case of a man's death according to Sharia, though, by the same code, men inherit twice as much as women.

Sports are permitted according to Sharia, and according to the hadith Muhammad specifically encouraged some, such as archery, horseback-riding, swimming, racing, and wrestling. However, certain games are prohibited, specifically ones related to gambling, such as cards and chance games using dice.

Sharia also mandates a manner of dress for both men and women, based on ideals of modesty. Traditionally, for men this has been interpreted as being covered from knee to neck. For women, interpretations and practice vary more. Under the strictest interpretation, women are obligated to cover their whole bodies, except for their hands and face. However, there is a claim by some modern feminists that the *hijab*, or headscarf, is not an actual Qur'anic injunction but rather a custom. Most major Islamic scholars today do not accept this view but some, most notably Jamal al-Banna, claim the hijab is not obligatory.

In the West, perhaps the most controversial aspect of Sharia is the sentencing mandated for certain crimes, referred to as *hadd* offenses, notably the provision that theft is punished by the amputation of one or both hands. However, according to Sharia, there is a high burden of proof for such crimes.

The Qur'an mandates specific punishments for hadd offenses: The consumption of alcohol is punished by flogging. Unlawful

In some Muslim countries, women are required to completely veil their faces, so that only their eyes are visible. Other countries take a more moderate approach, requiring women to wear headscarves and dress modestly.

sexual intercourse is punished by flogging for unmarried offenders and stoning for adulterers. False accusation of unlawful sexual intercourse is punished by flogging. Theft is punished by amputation. Highway robbery is punished by amputation or death, if the crime results in murder.

The adoption of these penalties as state laws has come to be seen as an expression of a country's Islamic identity, even if the punishments are not or are rarely carried out in practice. Islamists, however, generally support the use of such punishments.

Apostasy—the abandonment of Islam—is another situation punishable by death according to Sharia law. Although most Islamic countries no longer execute people who leave the faith, Islamists favor capital punishment for Muslims who have renounced their faith.

Sharia in Muslim Countries

A powerful state based on Sharia was the Ottoman Empire, which emerged in the early 1400s. Initially centered in the Anatolian Peninsula (modern-day Turkey), the Ottoman Empire controlled vast territories in the Middle East, North Africa, Central Asia, and Eastern Europe at its height in 1672. By the late 19th century, however, Western intellectual influences and the conquests of some Muslim majority regions led to a decline in the influence of Sharia.

During World War I (1914–1918), the Ottoman Empire was aligned with the Central Powers (Germany and Austria-Hungary). In 1919, after the war ended, the victorious Allied Powers (particularly France, Great Britain, and Italy) divided up the Ottoman territories to create new states, such as Iraq and Syria. The Allies controlled these states under the League of Nation's mandate system, in which the Western powers were

The modern state of Turkey was established in 1923 as a secular democracy. In recent years, however, Turkey's prime minister, Recep Erdogan, has been accused of attempting to allow Islam a greater role in Turkey's government and society.

expected to prepare them for independence. Over time, Arab states in the Middle East gained independence. Additionally, in 1923, the secular state of Turkey was established on the Anatolian Peninsula.

During the Ottoman period, local and regional governments of the Middle East had functioned under Sharia. As new states were created, reformers adopted large parts of Western legal systems as the basis for government. Many of these countries (Saudi Arabia being an exception) replaced Sharia and the role of scholarly Islamic opinion with state law. As a result, ritual matters and, to a lesser extent, personal status issues (such as marriage or divorce) remained in the hands of the Islamic legal scholars, but in most cases the state assumed authority for civil affairs.

Implementing Sharia

The Muslim community today can be divided into three sectors regarding Sharia and the authority of the state. Secularists believe that Sharia has no role in governing the state. Traditionalists believe that Sharia should be the main, but not only, source of law. Islamists advocate that Sharia be the law of the land.

Each of these influences can be seen in the various governments that have evolved in majority Muslim nations. In most Islamic countries Sharia influences the legal code to a certain extent, although there are some laws that are secular in origin. Each country's particular legal code and the role of Sharia

Between 1996 and 2001, an Islamist government called the Taliban ruled Afghanistan. The Taliban implemented an extremely strict version of Sharia law. Schools were closed and many forms of entertainment were banned. Religious police enforced the laws, and offenders were publicly beaten or executed. After U.S. troops helped to overthrow the Taliban government in late 2002, schools like this one in the Andar province of Afghanistan were reopened.

within it reflects a mix of political, historical, and cultural influences unique to that country.

On the secular end of the spectrum, Turkey is the most extreme, with a secular constitution and some laws that directly contradict Sharia. One of these laws is a particularly controversial measure that bans women in universities and government ministries from wearing headscarves. Other countries with secular constitutions and laws include Indonesia, Bangladesh, and Pakistan, and they have a few Islamic provisions regarding personal status laws.

On the traditionalist end of the spectrum are Iran, Saudi Arabia, and Afghanistan under the Taliban regime (1996–2001). In Iran, the mullahs (Muslims trained in Islamic theology and law) serve as the ultimate authority. They interpret what they believe to be the will of Allah for the laws governing the country. In Saudi Arabia the Qur'an serves as the constitution. The African countries of Libya and Sudan, as well as some states in Nigeria, also have many laws based directly on Sharia. A bill has been proposed in the Aceh province of Indonesia that would impose Sharia on everyone, even non-Muslims.

In the middle, most Muslim countries use Sharia as the basis of personal and family laws. In some countries, separate courts like the Muslim Personal Board in India or the Code of Muslim Personal Laws in the Philippines use Sharia laws to rule on matters regarding personal status. Malaysia has a mixed legal system, with a secular legal code, but in matters of personal and family law Muslims are subject to Islamic law. The rest of the population comes under civil law.

Countries in the Middle East and North Africa typically have a dual system in which the religious courts settle personal status issues and the secular courts have jurisdiction over all other matters. The exceptions to this are Saudi Arabia and Iran, where religious courts oversee all matters of jurisprudence.

The governments of many majority Muslim countries have limited traditional Qur'anic interpretations of punishment, rarely if ever invoking punishments such as floggings or amputations. In fact, only Saudi Arabia, Iran, and some states in Nigeria have formally instituted such penalties as state laws. In Pakistan, while these laws are also on the books, there is a parallel set of procedural laws that make it very difficult for Sharia punishments to be enforced by the courts.

The governments in some majority Muslim nations have replaced the Sharia criminal code with secular laws, while others have created laws based on the Sharia but that are more liberal in degree. Jordan, Kuwait, Yemen, and Pakistan are among the countries that have some laws based on traditional Islamic law. For example, the Qur'anic ban on alcohol has led these states to prohibit the sale of alcohol.

Even when Sharia is not explicitly enshrined in the national law, Islamic law is often maintained in governmental practices. For example, in many countries it is almost impossible for a Muslim to convert to another religion; committing apostasy is a punishable offense. Even in so-called secular countries, such as Egypt and Turkey, a Christian seeking to repair a church or build a new one can be hindered by the government.

In some countries aspects of Islamic finance and banking have been incorporated into legal codes. Traditional Sharia prohibits the charging of interest, earning excessive profits, or investing in enterprises that are inconsistent with Islamic law. Some countries try to act within these principles. Malaysia, for example, issues national bonds that are compliant with Sharia principles. Furthermore, eight Muslim countries—Malaysia, Indonesia, Iran, Saudi Arabia, Pakistan, Sudan, Bahrain, and Kuwait—are part of the Islamic Financial Services Board, which sets standards for Islamic banking.

The Palace of Justice in Putrajaya, Malaysia, houses the country's appellate and federal courts. Muslims with civil grievances can have their cases heard in the state's Sharia courts, which are located throughout Malaysia's 13 states.

In Muslim majority nations, there is pressure to make the legal system closer to or completely based on the principles of Sharia. Even when Sharia practices are not on the books, governments are usually reluctant to compel people to follow state law or to punish those who carry out practices based on Sharia.

Islamists

Followers of political Islamism believe that Sharia should serve as the basis for Muslim society in Muslim majority countries; any regions that have ever been ruled by Muslims; and, in some cases, the entire world. Their aim is to re-create a Muslim caliphate, a single government for all Muslim majority states that is based on Sharia.

Islamism is a militant movement, with followers taking up the cause of *jihad* (holy war) to achieve its aims. Islamist movements exist around the world and are active in non-Muslim majority countries as well as in predominantly Muslim ones. Islamist groups include the Sunni Muslim Brotherhood, founded in Egypt in 1928; Hizb ut-Tahrir, founded in 1953; and al-Qaeda, founded in 1988 by Osama bin Laden. Local organizations that are active in specific countries include the Palestinian group Hamas, founded in 1987 as a wing of Egypt's Muslim Brotherhood, and the Shia Islamist organization Hezbollah, founded in 1982 in Lebanon. These groups incorporate a wide range of tactics ranging from terrorism to intensive propaganda to charity work.

Aided by funding from Saudi Arabia, which follows Wahhabism, the Islamist movement has seen a resurgence in

The flag of the Lebanese Islamist organization Hezbollah, with its stylized script representing a hand holding an automatic rifle, illustrates the group's willingness to use violence to achieve its goals. The U.S. government considers Hezbollah a terrorist organization.

recent decades. Wahhabism is a school of Islam that not only adheres to Sharia as a legal code but also explicitly urges that all non-Muslim practices be avoided and that non-Muslims be forced to submit.

The Cairo Declaration

In addition to serving as the basis in varying degrees for the legal system in certain Muslim majority countries, Sharia is also the basis of the Cairo Declaration of Human Rights in Islam. This declaration originated with the Organization of the Islamic Conference (OIC), an association of Islamic states that works to promote Muslim solidarity in economics, social, and political affairs. The Cairo Declaration, which was adopted in 1990, provides the "official" Islamic perspective on human rights. It is the international Muslim community's answer to the UN Universal Declaration on Human Rights, which the OIC criticized for being too rooted in secular values.

Wahhabism

In the 18th century an extremely conservative form of Islam emerged in Saudi Arabia. It was developed by a religious scholar named Muhammad ibn Abd al-Wahhab, who preached that only the purest form of Sunni Islam was acceptable. He forged an alliance with Muhammad ibn Saud, the patriarch of a powerful family in central Arabia.

During the 20th century, a descendant of Ibn Saud's unified Arabia and established the state of Saudi Arabia. The country adopted Wahhabism as the official form of Islam. This Wahhabi ideology has led to the establishment of extremely strict Islamic laws in Saudi Arabia.

The Cairo Declaration opens by calling on the *umma* (Islamic nation) to assume responsibility for defending the rights enumerated within the declaration. The first of the document's 25 Articles acknowledges the equality of men, and it forbids discrimination based on race, color, language, belief, sex, religion, political affiliation, or social status.

Subsequent articles declare the sanctity of human life and the preservation thereof, based on Sharia. They proclaim the right of children to be provided for by their parents; for provisions to be made for children, women, the sick, and the elderly during war; and for people to have the right to their residences. Article 19 presumes innocence, guarantees a fair trial, and stipulates that the only punishments permitted are those specified by Sharia. Articles 20 and 21 protect people from being tortured or maltreated, and forbid the taking of hostages. Article 22 guarantees freedom of expression, although this right cannot be used to criticize the prophets of Islam or incite hatred or discrimination.

While the Cairo Declaration grants women several rights—including the right to marriage, equality to men in human dignity, and the right to financial independence—women are not granted equality to men in other areas. Article 6 states that the husband is responsible for the support and welfare of the family.

The Cairo Declaration upholds the principle of Sharia that Muslims cannot change religions. Furthermore, Muslims cannot be subjected to the rule of non-Muslims, although all Muslims are entitled to self-determination and must live under the rule of law. The final statement of the Cairo Declaration, Article 25, maintains that the Islamic Sharia is the only source of reference for the articles in the declaration.

Islam and Human Rights

Although most Muslim majority countries are not ruled entirely by Sharia, it is considered a source for lawmaking and governance. The legal systems in most Muslim countries are the result not only of religious ruling but also of historical and political traditions and cultural circumstances. Laws and practice concerning human rights also depend on all these factors and therefore vary across the Muslim world.

The following sections look at some human rights and how they have been viewed by general international practice, by Sharia, and in various Muslim majority countries. International practice is based on the standards established by the United Nations Universal Declaration on Human Rights.

Freedom of Religion: International Practice

The Universal Declaration of Human Rights guarantees equality to everyone regardless of his or her religion. It states that everyone has the right to freedom of thought, conscience, and religion. Each person has the right to practice his or her religion through worship, teaching, or other observances in public or in private. People also have the right to change their religion if they wish to do so.

Freedom of Religion: Sharia

According to Sharia, as it has been interpreted over the centuries, Muslims should always rule in countries that have large Muslim populations. Jihad, holy war, is an important principle in the Qur'an that implores Muslims to fight the non-believer and bring their lands under the control of Islam. Sharia does not support the concept that all religions should be treated equally.

In states governed in accordance with Sharia, Christianity and Judaism are tolerated religions, as opposed to polytheistic faiths,

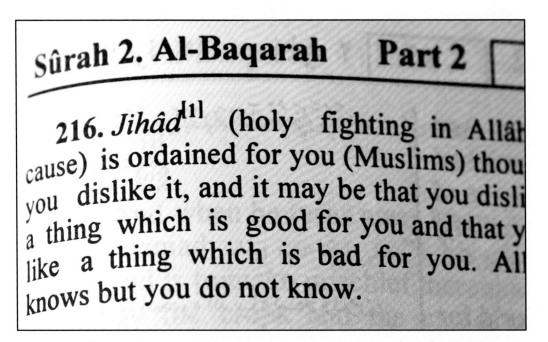

Sûrah 2. Al-Baqarah **Part 2**

216. *Jihâd*[1] (holy fighting in Allâh cause) is ordained for you (Muslims) thou you dislike it, and it may be that you disli a thing which is good for you and that y like a thing which is bad for you. All knows but you do not know.

The word *jihad* means "holy war" and is commonly used by Muslims to refer to conflict against unbelievers. Some Muslims claim that jihad can also refer to the struggle within each Muslim to live a moral life.

such as Hinduism and Buddhism, which are not allowed to exist at all. Jews and Christians, who are referred to as *dhimmis*, have fewer legal and social rights than Muslims.

Dhimmis were historically required to accept the primacy of Islam through defeat or surrender, submission, and payment of a special tax. They are restricted in their practices today, forbidden, for example, from building new places of worship or repairing old ones.

Some Muslim reformers or apologists have argued that certain Qur'anic verses support the idea of freedom of religion. They cite verses such as, "Let he who chooses to believe, believe, and he who chooses to disbelieve, disbelieve," and, "There is no compulsion in religion." This viewpoint has not been adopted, however, as mainstream Muslim doctrine. Generally, such verses were interpreted as rejecting the idea of forced conversion to Islam. However, adherents of other religions have historically been pressured to voluntarily convert to Islam in order to reap the social and financial benefits of becoming a Muslim.

Sharia maintains that apostasy—the abandonment of Islam—is punishable by death. Furthermore, the rights of non-Muslims or of Muslims who convert to another religion are not protected by Sharia law as they are in the Universal Declaration of Human Rights.

Freedom of Religion in Muslim Majority Countries

Article 18 of the Universal Declaration of Human Rights guarantees religious freedom, including the right to change one's religion or belief. This article has been one of the most controversial with many Muslims, who say it cannot be followed without breaking Islamic law.

The Cairo Declaration does not address equality of religions or the right to the freedom of religion. Instead it states, "Islam is the religion of true unspoiled nature." In line with Sharia, the Declaration notes that no one should be forced to change his religion, but it does not spell out specific rights to practice religion freely or to change religions.

In many Muslim majority states there have been human rights violations in the treatment of minority religions. In Pakistan, for example, the constitution guarantees religious freedom, yet Pakistani law contradicts this right, at least for the Ahmadiyya religious community. The Ahmadiyyas consider themselves Muslim, but many Muslims do not agree. Pakistani law has legalized discrimination against the group—its members cannot practice the faith publicly, distribute religious material, or build mosques. Under Pakistani law, practicing Ahmadiyya is a crime punishable by death.

Although there are civil laws in Egypt that provide for freedom of religious belief and practice, several minorities face ongoing discrimination. Members of the Copt Christian group, for example, have been prevented from practicing their religion, and have even been attacked and killed. The Egyptian regime has not been helpful in protecting Christians or in prosecuting their attackers. In November 2008, Christians in Cairo were unable to get a government license to build a church and so converted a warehouse into a house of worship. At the dedication of the building, thousands of Muslims attacked the church in the name of Islam. There was little police interference.

Since the 1979 Islamic revolution, the rule of Sharia has meant a lack of equality for members of other religions in Iran. The Iranian constitution guarantees a certain level of protection for Jews, Christians, and Zoroastrians. However, they are often targeted, accused of undertaking anti-Islamic activities. The religious faith of Baha'ism, like Ahmadiyya in Pakistan, is illegal in Iran. Baha'is have suffered serious persecution, including arrests, banning of activities, and confiscation of property.

Some Muslims within Muslim majority countries also suffer from a lack of equality. In Bahrain, which is ruled by Sunnis, the majority Shia population experiences widespread discrimination in education and employment. The

The exterior of a Coptic monastery in Egypt. The Copts are one of the oldest Christian sects, originating in the decades after the death of Jesus. Today, Copts are the largest Christian group in North Africa. However, they have faced opposition and discrimination by Islamists in Egypt and other countries.

same applies to the Shia in Saudi Arabia, where they are a minority.

The governments of Saudi Arabia and Iran have punished apostasy with imprisonment or death. In Egypt, families that have converted to Islam, and then decided to convert back to Christianity have been refused the right to officially identify themselves as Christians on their identification cards. In Malaysia, the government has imprisoned some people who wished to convert, discriminated against converts in divorce or inheritance cases, and even declared some people as converts to Islam, despite their denials to that claim. The government automatically identifies their children as Muslim, regardless of their parents' wishes.

Freedom of Expression: International Practice

The Universal Declaration of Human Rights states that everyone has the right to freedom of opinion and expression. All people also have the right to seek, receive, and impart information and ideas through any media. This freedom of expression applies to individuals and also to the media and other organizations.

Freedom of Expression: Sharia

While moderate and reform-minded Muslims assert that the Qur'an permits freedom of opinion and expression, this is not the way it is widely interpreted. Most fundamentalist Muslims believe that Sharia prohibits any criticism of Islam or its main tenets. Similarly, any questioning of the Qur'an, which fundamentalists view as God's Word, is defined as sacrilege.

Freedom of Expression in Muslim Majority Countries

In many Muslim majority countries, freedom of expression is severely restricted. The Cairo Declaration limits freedom of

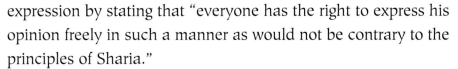

expression by stating that "everyone has the right to express his opinion freely in such a manner as would not be contrary to the principles of Sharia."

The regimes in many Muslim countries heavily restrict the media's freedom. Organizations concerned with freedom of the press frequently list Muslim countries in the Arab world as some of the worst offenders on this issue. Freedom of expression is most often restricted for political reasons and due to the nature of the government rather than for religious reasons. However, the only reason Sharia doesn't come into play more often as a factor is that most people in cultural and intellectual fields exercise pervasive self-censorship.

In many Muslim countries, such as Egypt, the government exerts strict control over what people are allowed to read in newspapers or watch on television.

A regime that had imposed Islamic law in Sudan executed a dissident moderate Muslim scholar in 1985. In other countries the authors of song lyrics that used Qur'anic passages, even in a clearly respectful way, faced threats of judicial persecution.

The Internet poses new challenges to the tight control many regimes exercise. Several countries have heavily restricted its use. In Egypt and Syria, people who have written blogs criticizing the government or publicizing human rights' violations have been imprisoned.

While limitations on freedom of expression commonly occur in corrupt, non-democratic regimes, some restrictions are due to Sharia injunctions, whether legally mandated in state law or merely highly influential. As a result, serious intellectual work in Islamic history and theology, archaeology, linguistic analysis of early Muslim history, and other fields has been limited to the point of being eliminated.

In a case in Egypt, Islamists claimed a scholar whose findings contradicted traditional interpretations was not a "proper" Muslim. In a court case, they demanded the annulment of the man's marriage. When the court upheld the suit, the man and his wife fled the country.

In Saudi Arabia it is legally forbidden to criticize Islam. Even articles that attack extremists were banned after the subjects of the stories charged that the negative remarks referred to Islamic practice in general.

Differences between the West and Muslim majority countries over freedom of expression came to the attention of the West after Danish newspapers, citing the right of freedom of the press, published cartoons of the prophet Muhammad in late 2005. The depictions of the prophet Muhammad, which Muslims reject as a form of idolatry, set off violent protests in many Muslim majority countries. While Western society supports the rights of people to protest what they consider to be offensive, society does not permit violence or limits on freedom of speech.

Through the United Nations and other international organizations, Muslim majority states have tried to establish restrictions that define sacrilege as a crime, mainly in instances when Muslims pronounced a given expression offensive to their religion. Aside from the restrictions on freedom in general, the definition of "offense" is often so flexible as to impinge on legitimate scholarship and criticism.

Equality of Women: International Practice

The Universal Declaration of Human Rights applies to all men and women equally. For example, women should be able to vote, receive equal pay for equal work, and have inheritance or divorce rights equal to those of men.

Equality of Women: Sharia

The status of women under Sharia law differs in many ways to their status under the Universal Declaration of Human Rights and in Western countries. Islam spells out distinctly different roles for men and women, with men as the masters of society and family. Muslim reformers and feminists often deny this. They cite Qur'anic verses that they say stress women's equality. For example, Sura 4:124 states, "And whosoever does deeds of righteousness, be it male or female, believing—they shall enter Paradise and not be wronged."

However, other verses have a different message. Sura 2:228 declares, "Men stand a step above them." In marriage, women should show obedience to their husbands and in some circumstances, the Qur'an permits men to hit wives whose behavior displeases them.

A man may divorce his wife easily and without cause, but the circumstances under which a woman is allowed to seek a divorce are far more limited. In divorce, the man is awarded custody of the children unless they are very young.

Women are also unequal to men in the matter of inheritance. Although women have inheritance rights when a male member of the family dies, men are entitled to double the inheritance of women.

Equality of Women in Muslim Majority Countries

The issue of women's rights is one area in which Sharia law remains highly influential in many Muslim countries. Sharia authority has had a negative effect on women's treatment in marriage, education, and work.

Even though the constitutions of some countries explicitly affirm the equality of women, such equality does not always exist. There are often laws based on Sharia that contradict the constitution. For example, Pakistan's constitution guarantees equality between men and women. However, a set of laws known as the Hudood Ordinances, passed in 1979 and amended in 2006, severely limit the rights of women. The ordinances implemented Sharia penalties in punishing adultery and sex outside marriage. These laws particularly affected women, making rape victims liable for prosecution and imprisoning them for having illegal sexual relationships.

In some countries, the equality of women is limited because there are no sufficient laws protecting women. Bahrain has no codified laws regulating matters such as marriage and divorce. Personal status rulings are therefore made by religious judges who decide cases based on Sharia. These rulings make no pretense of defending women's equality and consistently favor men.

In many countries, women suffer great inequality within marriage. In Iran the legal age for a girl to marry is 13 years old, whereas a boy must be age 15. Under Sharia law polygamy is permitted for men but not for women. And while polygamy is banned in Tunisia and Turkey, it remains legal in other Muslim countries.

Divorce is another area in which women have only limited rights. In Egypt the legal system discriminates against women who seek divorce. While a man does not even have to go to court when he wishes to divorce his wife, a woman faces a far more difficult process. In order to obtain full financial rights, she must prove that she has been harmed by her husband. This is often impossible to do. Thus, a woman who divorces typically receives no financial protection. Some women, frightened by the consequences of leaving, remain in unhappy marriages.

The strict Islamic laws followed in Saudi Arabia extremely limit many rights for women. The strict segregation of men and women means that women are provided with educational facilities and opportunities unequal to those of Saudi men. Most women's lives are totally regulated by a male guardian—a father, husband, or other male family member. A woman must obtain permission from her guardian before making most decisions. She may not leave the house without a male escort, who must be a member of her family.

Additional Saudi laws prohibit women from driving, meeting alone with men who are not close relatives, and traveling abroad without permission from a male member of the family. The same laws mean women cannot have equal rights in the workplace. Employers are often reluctant to hire women because they are also prohibited from interaction with male colleagues or clients and with certain agencies and officials.

In Islamic countries, women typically do not have rights equal to men.

Women face the threat of death if accused of behavior deemed to violate Islamic norms. While moderate Muslims or apologists argue that honor killings do not relate to Islam, the perpetrators of such crimes say they are following the teachings of their clerics. In Jordan and other countries, the killer's belief that he is defending the family's honor or acting to defend Islam can be a factor that courts take into account in reducing sentences. Women have been killed when suspected of sexual intimacy or for marrying or even meeting a man without family approval.

Fair Trials, Freedom from Torture: International Practice

The Universal Declaration of Human Rights states that everyone is entitled to a fair and speedy trial. People cannot be subject to arbitrary arrest or imprisoned indefinitely. Everyone is equal before the law and entitled to legal representation. People should be presumed innocent until proven guilty. Punishments for crimes should not be cruel or degrading and no one should be tortured.

Fair Trials, Freedom from Torture: Sharia

Sharia calls for justice to be delivered according to the principles of Islam and the will of Allah. Human legislators or judges cannot overturn the divine will, which is interpreted by clerics.

Sharia courts differ in many ways from those of the West. Trials in Sharia courts rely more heavily on the testimony of witnesses and put less weight on written or other forms of evidence. A woman may testify but her evidence counts for only half the value of a man's testimony. In other words, the testimony of two women equals that of one man.

Punishments traditionally enforced in Sharia courts are considered torture according to international standards. The Qur'an describes specific sentences for a group of offenses known as hadd crimes. The punishments include flogging for those found guilty of drinking alcohol, amputation of a hand for theft, and stoning to death for adultery.

Fair Trials, Freedom from Torture in Muslim Majority Countries

Most Muslim countries do not apply Sharia to criminal law. Secular laws are used instead, and hadd punishments are not implemented. The Cairo Declaration, like the Universal Declaration of Human Rights, states that everyone is equal before the law and innocent until proven guilty. The Cairo Declaration also forbids arbitrary arrest and torture. However, the document states, "There shall be no crime or punishment except as provided for in the Sharia." In other words, punishments as described in the Sharia, by definition, cannot be considered torture.

Torture is reportedly commonplace in most Arab countries, including ones where representatives signed the UN Convention Against Torture and Other Cruel, Inhuman or Degrading Treatment or Punishment (a convention calling on nations to prevent torture within their borders). Arbitrary arrests and detention without trial are also frequent. Governments make use of such practices to curb opposition by instilling fear and to eliminate dissident groups or other critics.

Sharia allows for the use of the death penalty for minors, which is a particularly controversial issue for Western observers. Countries using this punishment are Muslim majority states with high levels of Sharia influence in law: Iran, Saudi Arabia, Yemen, Pakistan, and Sudan. The governments of these countries justify the practice by defining an adult as anyone who has reached puberty. In Iran, girls are defined as being at "the age of majority" at only nine years old and boys at fifteen, as defined by Sharia provisions.

In Iran, Saudi Arabia, and parts of Nigeria, the criminal justice system is based on Sharia law. Hadd punishments are still used, although not frequently and with a high level of proof required. Still, in Muslim areas in Nigeria, women have been flogged for committing adultery. The punishment of stoning has also been ordered. In Saudi Arabia, flogging, amputation, and decapitation are used. The punishment of stoning to death for adultery continues, and it is almost always applied to women.

In countries where a strict version of Sharia law is enforced, such as Saudi Arabia, Nigeria, Sudan, and Iran, those who commit sexual crimes, such as rape or adultery, may be punished by stoning.

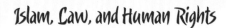

Free and Fair Elections: International Practice

Under the Universal Declaration of Human Rights, everyone has the right to take part in the government of his or her country, either directly or indirectly, through the election of a representative. The government of a country should reflect the people's will, with free and fair elections held regularly.

Free and Fair Elections: Sharia

Islam, as it has been interpreted throughout history, provides no one system of government, and over time the regimes ruling Muslim majority states have varied widely. There are, however, core principles that most Muslims believe governments must uphold. Muslims, of course, can disagree with this formulation but in doing so they are accepting, implicitly, an alternative viewpoint.

Most importantly, it is Allah—and not the government, ruler, or parliament—who holds supreme authority. Therefore, only God has the authority to make laws, and they have been given to Muslims in the Qur'an. Where no clear law is given, it is the responsibility of religiously trained legal experts to interpret God's will.

In some countries of the Arab world, such as Saudi Arabia, a Majlis al-Shura (counsultative council) is formed to advise the ruler. These assemblies are typically composed of elected officials or tribal leaders. However, the rulers have the final say in matters of law and legal interpretation.

As Allah is considered the supreme authority, the Muslim leader must fulfill God's will, whereas in Western democracies the will of the people is primary. Muslims who take the former stance consider this system most representative and fair because they believe that the Qur'an embodies equality. According to this concept, only a leader who implements God's will should hold high office—not someone elected by a majority of the people.

Consultation in government, however, is also a key principle in Islam. Rulers must consult with the people. This process is open to interpretation and takes a variety of forms. In traditional tribal societies, a shaikh consults with members of the tribe or their representatives. In modern societies, most Muslims interpret consultation as voting and the necessity of electing leaders or assemblies, although some Islamists oppose elections in principle.

After the death of Muhammad, the Muslim world was led by a caliph. In the centuries that followed, the nature of the caliphate changed greatly from supreme religious and political ruler to simply a religious authority, becoming an auxiliary title held by an essentially secular emperor, or sultan. The post of caliph was maintained until it was finally abolished after the Ottoman Empire was dissolved. Today, no such institution exists but Islamist organizations favor reestablishment of the caliphate as a transnational ruler with the powers of a dictator.

Free and Fair Elections: Muslim Majority Countries

The Cairo Declaration states that everyone is entitled to participate in the administration of his or her country and also to hold office in accordance with the provisions of Sharia. Throughout the Muslim world there are a variety of systems of government ranging from republics to hereditary monarchies. The extent to which they achieve democracy and the way

This Kurdish-language poster on a wall in Mosul, Iraq, encourages people to vote in provincial elections. Article 2 of Iraq's constitution, adopted in 2005 after the fall of Saddam Hussein, declares that "Islam is the official religion of the State and it is a fundamental source of legislation."

in which governments represent and suppress their people also varies greatly. These differences do not simply depend on Islam.

Muslim governments have changed greatly throughout history because of political factors, foreign domination, and the power of particular leaders. The repressive policies and lack of fair and free elections in many countries is best explained by governments that are unwilling to compromise their power and tolerate opposition.

Elections of some form are held in all Muslim majority countries. However even in more open states, elections have not always been free and fair, and they have often failed to guarantee representation. Jordan, Iran, and Egypt—respectively a constitutional monarchy, Islamist republic, and constitutional republic—all have multiparty systems and elections that in many ways appear fair. However, the manipulation of voting districts, questionable vote-counting, restrictions on who can run, and other factors guarantee a result pleasing to the incumbent regime. In Egypt, one legal provision blocks any party from participating in elections if it defines itself as religious—a successful effort that has reduced the Muslim Brotherhood's power.

Even when radical Islamist groups participate in elections, they may use balloting as a way to gain power in order to never relinquish it. Hamas won the 2005 Palestinian elections, and then used that success as a way to seize full power in the Gaza Strip and repress its opponents. In contrast, however, the more moderate, albeit Islamist-rooted, Justice and Development Party (AKP) took power in Turkey in 2002 and has maintained democratic elections and general human rights since then.

The Islamic Republic of Iran provides a unique example of Islamist rule combined with parliamentary elections and repressive policies. Iran has a supreme guide, who is always a Muslim cleric, as the country's chief executive, and two high-level councils, dominated by clerics, which pass on the Sharia validity of all legislation. Thus, while reformists won several elections by wide margins, including that of a two-term president, they were unable to enact a single change. The cleric-dominated councils also can veto the candidacy of anyone for parliament. Any party or individual not deemed supportive of Islamist rule in Iran would be disqualified and, most likely, arrested.

In Iran, the Grand Ayatollah Ali Khameni has been able to thwart efforts by reformers to moderate the country's Islamist government policies.

In all issues related to human rights, the policy of Muslim majority countries is influenced by numerous factors. In some cases Sharia law directly defines practice but far more often it is a country's regime and its political traditions that determine the level of respect for human rights or abuse of them. At the same time, though, it should be noted that Sharia has tremendous indirect power because it sets the norms and boundaries of what is accepted in society and by government in virtually all Muslim majority countries.

While regimes in the past—particularly in the first three-quarters of the 20th century—gradually reduced the influence of Sharia, since the 1970s that trend has been reversed. If Islamist groups succeed in seizing power in any country, Sharia will be further strengthened not only in that place but also—through Islamist pressure, regime fear, and the rulers' trying to bolster their own Islamic credentials—throughout the Muslim majority world.

A final consideration is the extent to which Sharia spreads as a sub-system in the West. For example, in Canada, the United Kingdom, and other European countries, elements of Sharia in the handling of personal status law for Muslims have been introduced. The key areas in this respect are matters of marriage, divorce, and free speech.

The way in which the pressures of pragmatism, modernity, the needs of the existing regimes, revolutionary pressure, and cultural-intellectual diffusion from the West are managed and balanced in each country will determine the future power of Sharia and the extent of human rights.

Chronology

570: Muhammad is born in Mecca.

610: The first revelation of the Qu'ran to Muhammad.

632: The death of Muhammad; the Qu'ran is codified and the post of caliph is established; Islam begins expanding beyond Arabia.

1215: The Magna Carta is signed by King John of England; it gives his subjects certain rights and is a fundamental step in the development of a system of rights enshrined in law and protected by institutions.

1453: The Ottomans conquer Constantinople (Istanbul), which becomes the capital of the new Islamic Empire.

1516–17: The Ottoman Empire expands to include Syria, Egypt and western Arabia.

1776: The Declaration of Independence, which proclaims equality and the rights to life, liberty, and the pursuit of happiness for all men, is signed in the United States.

1789: The Declaration of the Rights of Man and of the Citizen in France proclaims quality, liberty, property, and resistance to oppression; the U.S. Bill of Rights guarantees specific rights in the United States.

Late 1800s: The status of Sharia recedes with the decline of Ottoman Empire and the adoption of Western legal systems in countries throughout the Muslim world.

1923: The secular state of Turkey is established.

1924: The caliphate is abolished.

1948: The Universal Declaration of Human Rights is adopted by the General Assembly of the United Nations; it proclaims certain basic rights like freedom and equality for everyone regardless of race, sex, religion, or political opinion.

1979: The Iranian Revolution leads to the establishment of the Islamic Republic of Iran, which implements Sharia; Hudood Ordinances enacted in Pakistan.

1985: The Convention Against Torture is drafted.

1989: The Convention on the Rights of the Child is drafted.

1990: The Cairo Declaration of Human Rights in Islam is adopted as the answer to the UN Declaration on Human Rights, proclaiming certain rights based on Sharia.

2000–2004: Sharia criminal law adopted in 12 northern states of Nigeria, increasing tensions between Muslims and Christians.

2008: United Kingdom House of Lords declares Sharia incompatible with UK human rights legislation.

2009: In a peace deal with the Taliban, Pakistan agrees to implementation of Sharia in the country's tribal region of Swat Valley.

Glossary

caliph—a successor to Muhammad who was originally both the religious and political leader of Muslims; later the post was only a religious title.

civil law—body of laws established by a nation for its own regulation.

common law—part of English law derived from custom and previous decisions of courts.

convention—a legally binding agreement between states.

declaration—a document stating agreed-upon standards or norms but that is not legally binding.

hadd—offense listed in the Qu'ran for which the punishments are outlined by Sharia; hadd crimes and penalties include flogging for consumption of alcohol, hand amputation for theft, and stoning to death for adultery.

hadith—the collection of sayings and actions of Muhammad.

Hudood Ordinances—a set of laws in Pakistan that severely limits the rights of women by criminalizing adultery and extramarital sex.

human rights—the rights to life, freedom, equality before the law, and justice. Human rights are considered to be universal and therefore are for all people no matter where they live and no matter their religion, gender, or race.

ijma—scholarly consensus on matters not directly addressed by the Qu'ran or hadith.

ijtihad—an Islamic tenet by which qualified scholars interpret Muslim law through analysis and logic.

Islamism—a political philosophy that seeks to attain state power in order to create a society in which all Islam, according to the interpretation of the movement, is supreme in all matters.

jihad—a holy war against non-Muslims.

jurisprudence—the theory or philosophy of law.

qiyas—legal analogy; a tool used by Islamic jurists to derive Sharia.

Qu'ran—Islam 's holy scriptures, a key source of Islamic law and practice.

Sharia—Islamic law.

Wahhabism—a conservative form of Islam practiced in Saudi Arabia and Qatar that insists on a literal interpretation of the Qu'ran and regards all people with different views, including Muslims, as enemies of Islam.

Further Reading

Bakhtiar, Laleh and Kevin Reinhart. *Encyclopedia of Islamic Law: A Compendium of the Major Schools.* Chicago: Kazi Publications, 1996.

Feldman, Noah, "Why Shariah?" *New York Times*, March 16, 2008.

Littman, David G., "Human Rights and Human Wrongs," *National Review Online*, January 19, 2003.

Internet Resources

http://www.bbc.co.uk/religion

A discussion of Islam and Sharia can be found on this BBC Web site about religion and ethics.

http://www.cfr.org/publication/8034

Council on the Council on Foreign Relations publication Backgrounder provides information in the article "Islam: Governing Under Sharia."

http://www.religlaw.org/interdocs/docs/cairohrislam1990.htm

The Cairo Declaration on Human Rights in Islam.

#

Numbers in **bold italics** refer to captions.